PHONETICS FO[R PHONICS]

/fəˈnetɪks fə ˈfɒnɪks/

Underpinning Knowledge for Adult Literacy Practitioners

Maxine Burton

21 De Montfort Street
Leicester LE1 7GE

Company registration no. 2603322

Charity registration no. 1002775

NIACE has a broad remit to promote lifelong learning opportunities for adults. NIACE works to develop increased participation in education and training, particularly for those who do not have easy access because of class, gender, age, race, language and culture, learning difficulties or disabilities, or insufficient financial resources.

For a full catalogue of all NIACE's publications visit

http://shop.niace.org.uk/

Cataloguing in Publications Data
A CIP record for this title is available from the British Library

ISBN 978 1 86201 453 4

Designed and typeset by Book Production Services

Contents

Acknowledgements

My thanks are owed to:

- NIACE for the invitation to give a presentation on phonics in March 2009 at their Leicester headquarters and for subsequently encouraging me to write this book;
- Greg Brooks, Emeritus Professor of Education, University of Sheffield, for all the tables in Appendix 3 and for his expert advice throughout, especially regarding phonics for spelling; and
- The National Research and Development Centre for Adult Literacy and Numeracy (NRDC) at the Institute of Education, University of London, for funding the research projects on which this book draws, and for providing me, as Visiting Research Associate, with the use of a desk and research facilities during the writing of it.

Introduction

The genesis of this book lies in a combination of factors: my decades of experience as an adult literacy teacher; my long-standing interest in and teaching of linguistics, particularly phonetics and phonology of English; and, most significantly, the insights gained from an NRDC project I directed at the University of Sheffield, 2007–08 (Burton *et al.*, 2008, 2010). This research project not only aimed to assess the effectiveness of phonics in the adult literacy classroom, but included, as an essential part of the methodology, training of teachers over several sessions to prepare them to deliver phonics in the classroom.

In the absence of any phonics schemes and materials specifically for adults, and therefore no clear guidelines as to how to set about using phonics systematically with adults, I thought it important to give the teachers a thorough grounding in the basics of phonetics. This underpinning knowledge would give them the confidence to adapt existing phonics schemes for children to suit their learners, and the flexibility to deal with learners' queries as they arose. Above all, it was intended to ensure that their phonics teaching was accurate and consistent.

How to use this book

To a great extent, this book is informed by the four training sessions I designed for the teachers who participated in the above project and, importantly, by the feedback from them. Although the study of phonetics formed the backbone of the training – and will provide the main focus of this book – the aim is to de-mystify it as a subject, and relate this knowledge to what teachers need for phonics in the classroom. This is not a phonetics textbook, although you will be taught all the key terms and concepts you need. Nor is it, in any sense, a 'how to teach phonics' book – that topic will have to be addressed elsewhere.

It is probably better to work through the chapters in turn, although they are grouped into sections. The first two provide background: a brief rationale of phonics as a strategy; and why phonetics matters for phonics. The next two, Chapters 3 and 4, deal with the International Phonetic Alphabet (IPA) and the basic principles of English phonetics and phonology. Chapters 5 and 6 suggest ways of linking phonetics knowledge to teaching in the classroom using the framework of the Adult Literacy Core Curriculum. Chapter 7 explores the related issue of different accents of English. Each chapter has suggestions for further reading and the two chapters on phonetics and the IPA incorporate some 'tasks' (with answers) to engage the reader. A full list of references can be found at the end, followed by a glossary of all linguistic terms used.

Chapter 1
Why phonics for adults?

By 'phonics' we mean an approach to teaching reading and spelling which focuses on the association of phonemes (speech sounds) with particular graphemes (letters or groups of letters). This relationship between sounds and letters is the basis of whichever type of phonics (synthetic or analytic) is involved. We shall examine in more detail in later chapters exactly what these concepts entail and these, and all other linguistic terms used, are listed in the glossary at the end of the book. There has been renewed interest in phonics over the past few years, at least as far as initial literacy is concerned, with the findings of the Rose Review (Rose, 2006) and the incorporation of phonics into the National Literacy Strategy (later the Primary National Strategy). There is strong research evidence that systematic phonics instruction, within a broad and rich literacy curriculum, enables children to make better progress in word identification than unsystematic or no phonics instruction. This finding rests on two systematic reviews of the research evidence, one in the US (Ehri *et al.*, 2001), the other in the UK (Torgerson *et al.*, 2006).

Prior to the recent major NRDC research referred to in the Introduction, little attention had been paid in the UK to the potential of phonics instruction for adults. Indeed, there has in the past been some reluctance on the part of adult literacy practitioners and teacher-trainers to engage with phonics. Certainly at the time we conducted our research (which will be referred to from now on as 'the Phonics Project') few adult literacy training courses seemed to give much guidance on this strategy. However, if you're reading this book you must at least be interested in using phonics, so I won't labour the arguments for phonics or against other approaches.

Phonics is the most reliable method of word identification. What it can offer, over and above other strategies, is an approach that goes to the heart of how the English alphabetic system works. And English is an alphabetic language, albeit one that lacks as many one-to-one correspondences as other languages such as Finnish or Italian. There is more regularity than is often appreciated (a point which will become clearer in later chapters).

Adults who have learnt to recite the letters of the alphabet may still have failed to make the vital connection between the marks on the page and the sounds they represent, despite perhaps having memorised a good stock of sight vocabulary. Indeed, they may have mastered some correspondences but not others, a sometimes unexpected situation, referred to by one practitioner as 'pockets of missing information', e.g. not realising that the sequence <igh> has only one sound (Burton, 2007, p.12). Even learners who are able to 'sound out' the letters, in the sense of connecting certain letters with certain sounds, may still struggle to blend these sounds into words. This is a very specific skill and to the beginner reader it is not immediately obvious. For example, during one class observation in the course of the Phonics Project, it was noted that an Entry 1 learner, who could name the letters of the alphabet in a word, and sound them out individually, was unable, without further help, to take this knowledge one step further and realise that these sounds should then be blended to make words.

There is more to phonics teaching than getting learners to associate certain sounds with certain letters – the crucial part is training to blend (or segment for spelling). Is it so surprising that the sequence of sounds, 'kuh', 'a', 'tuh', do not automatically resolve themselves into the word 'cat'?

If word recognition is a prerequisite for the ultimate goal of comprehension, then it seems perverse to withhold or downgrade knowledge of phonic techniques as a useful first step in decoding, and thus empowering learners to become independent readers. I believe strongly that phonics should be the first (but not the only) word identification strategy used, a point that was also made in the Rose Review recommendations (Rose, 2006).

The Phonics Project mentioned above showed that many negative attitudes to phonics needed to be re-examined. Our findings indicated that it is a strategy that should be taken seriously for adult literacy learners. The 52, mainly Entry level, learners who participated made significant gains in their reading comprehension and spelling, and also in their confidence across a range of literacy skills, within, on average, only five to six sessions of phonics instruction. Most of the teachers expressed enthusiasm for phonics as suitable for a wide range of learners, and stated their intention to continue using it in the classroom. It seemed to be a popular strategy with the majority of the learners, who gave positive feedback in terms of increased motivation and enjoyment (and did not find it particularly 'babyish'). Although our teachers and learners were not required to follow a set phonics scheme, we did recommend the DCSF framework, *Letters and Sounds*, available free or downloadable from **http://nationalstrategies.standards.dcsf.gov.uk/node/84969**.

If we are going to take phonics seriously, then we also need to take the training of teachers seriously. Although seemingly not in wholehearted favour of phonics, Hughes & Schwab (2010, p.168) do agree that the key to successful phonics teaching is 'informed teachers'. What this might involve is the topic of the next chapter.

If you want to find out more:

Burton, M., Davey, J., Lewis, M., Ritchie, L. and Brooks, G. (2008) *Improving Reading: Phonics and Fluency. Practitioner Guide*. London: NRDC.

The first half of this guide (pp.8–31) gives guidelines and resources for using phonics in the adult literacy classroom, based on the 2007–08 phonics project. It can also be downloaded from: **www.nrdc.org.uk/publications_details.asp?ID=156**

Burton, M., Davey, J., Lewis, M., Ritchie, L. and Brooks, G. (2010) *Progress for adult literacy learners.* London: NRDC

This gives a full account of the methods and findings of the above research project and is only available online (free download) at: **www.nrdc.org.uk/publications_details.asp?ID=175#**

Burton, M. (2007) *Reading. Developing adult teaching and learning: practitioner guides.* Leicester: NIACE.

This was written in consultation with practitioners and teacher-trainers and sets phonics (pp.12–14) within the general context of reading.

Finally, a 2009 *Education Guardian* article by Peter Kingston, entitled *Can you teach an old dog with young tricks?* presents the case for and against the use of phonics with adults: **www.guardian.co.uk/education/2009/apr/14/literacy-adult-education-phonics**

Chapter 2

Why does phonetics matter for phonics?

Research has shown that phonics instruction needs to be systematic, not half-hearted or *ad hoc*. It needs to be accurate. Inaccurate phonics is misleading and unhelpful for the learner. There are many examples of misguided phonics in classroom practice, observed over the years (see Besser *et al.*, 2004; Brooks *et al.*, 2007; Burton *et al.*, 2008, 2010). Accurate and systematic phonics teaching requires a good underpinning knowledge of the phonetics and phonology (the study of the individual sounds and sound system) of English. Although current training requirements do now include English language and linguistics, a recent publication (Howard and Kings, 2010) points out that, with many teachers having entered the profession through earlier routes (e.g. the City & Guilds volunteer qualifications), minimal linguistic knowledge is regrettably common. 'It has always been a surprise to find out how little the majority of teachers know about how language works and, even more surprising, to find that phonology is usually a complete mystery... Few know how to teach a non-reader to read' (Howard and Kings, 2010, p.61). In the past it had been falsely assumed that anyone with a reasonable level of literacy themselves could teach literacy, especially to beginner learners, but nothing could be further from the truth. Beginner readers and writers above all need highly skilled teaching from teachers who are totally secure in their knowledge of language.

Teaching skills aside, surely an educated, literate native speaker knows enough about their language? Being a native speaker – or even a highly fluent second-language speaker – is no automatic guarantee of having a fully developed phonemic awareness, that is, an accurate understanding of the sounds of English. Indeed, some of the misleading phonics examples, arising from an incomplete understanding of the phonology of English, owe their existence to literacy on the part of the teacher! Consider the following examples, taken from practice observed in the course of NRDC projects between 2002 and 2008:

> *Trying to help a learner read the word <ship> by pointing out the /h/ 'sound'*
>
> *Breaking down the word <married> into 'syllables' – marr-i-ed- to make it easier to read*
>
> *Helping a learner spell the last letter of <floor> by asking what sound there was at the end of the word*

None of these examples accurately reflect the way the words sound. It is as though the teachers had been transfixed by the spelling to the extent that they have stopped really listening – victims of their own literacy. Even a recent book, focusing on spelling systems (Brunswick *et al.*, 2010), states that in words such as 'light' and 'sight' the sound /t/ is represented by the grapheme <ght>. A moment's thought, and comparison with words such as 'site' and 'sigh', would suggest a different correspondence. What training in phonetics and phonology can do is allow teachers to approach their language with fresh ears and fresh understanding. Knowledgeable teachers are confident teachers, able to adapt resources and methods as needed, and go with the 'teachable moment'. This is the case for all literacy teachers, but especially so for adult literacy practitioners who need to be flexible enough to deal competently with adult learners' often unpredictable queries and long-term misunderstandings. Adults are not beginners in the use of their language and, to repeat a familiar statement, 'A beginner reader is not a beginner thinker.'

If you want to find out more:

Bloomer, A., Griffiths, P. and Merrison, A. J. (2005) *Introducing Language in Use: A coursebook.* London: Routledge - two short sections - *Why is language worth studying?* (pp.7–8), and the *Introduction* to their chapter on phonetics (pp.230–2). (However, adult literacy teachers are not mentioned.)

Chapter 3

The International Phonetic Alphabet (IPA) explained

Before setting out the basics of phonetics and phonology, it is essential at this point to introduce you to the transcription system known as the International Phonetic Alphabet, or IPA. This is the normal medium through which phonetics is taught, and even the most 'back to basics' accounts of language for 'lay' audiences adopt the IPA without prior justification, e.g. David Crystal's *How Language Works* (2005). I must make it clear that this system is for the use of teachers, not for learners. Further necessary linguistic definitions will be given in the next chapters and referenced in the Glossary, but for now, note that the conventional way of representing sounds (phonemes) is between slanted brackets // and letters (graphemes), i.e. the written forms, within angled brackets<>. This may seem rather technical, but is far less confusing than using inverted commas ' ' for both or either.

The IPA is a system that was devised over 100 years ago. Within it, every single sound of any and every language can be represented by a symbol that provides a consistent one-to-one correspondence. For a language like English with its 26 letters of the alphabet and around 44 phonemes, there are obvious advantages. It is by far the best way of avoiding inconsistencies and ambiguities. The set of symbols for English, for the accent known as RP ('Received Pronunciation', 'BBC English'), is given in the two tables in Appendix 1 and is the same as that used in the phonetics training sessions in the Phonics Project (Burton *et al.*, 2008, 2010). For illustrative purposes, the first column, 'L&S', shows the symbols used in the phonics framework mentioned in the previous chapter, *Letters and Sounds* (where they are different from IPA). The L&S version, using only the 26 letters of the alphabet, plus /ə/ (known as schwa), singly or in combination, is based on one possible spelling of each English phoneme. It is one of the better non-IPA alternatives, but is not without some potential ambiguities.

It seems surprising, in view of its advantages, that IPA seems to be hardly ever used as part of the training in using such schemes. A welcome exception is the inclusion, in the Glossary to the online Adult Core Curricula, of a version of the IPA symbols for English, under the heading, 'phonemic alphabet'. This is also reproduced here as Appendix 2, and its choice of 46 symbols rather than the more conventional 44 will be discussed in the following chapter. However, despite its presence in the Glossary, there is no further reference to IPA within the curriculum. This is disappointing as it is a valuable tool in the phonics teacher's toolkit.

Task 1

Look at the IPA consonant list in Appendix 1 – how many are actually used with their familiar sound values?

(Answer at the end of this chapter)

To appreciate the flexibility of IPA, try going to the Speech Accent Archive at **http://accent.gmu.edu**. This American resource contains recordings of the same short English passage read in a variety of different accents, all with phonetic transcriptions using IPA. The issue of different accents of English will be revisited in Chapter 7.

When I teach face to face, I ask my students, at this stage, to have a go at transcribing their own names, using the IPA. Although I will be unable to comment on your versions, you might like to try this and see how far removed your name would be from 'normal' spelling. For example, <Sam> and <Samantha> become /sæm/ and /səˈmænθə/. (Capitals for 'proper nouns' are not used in IPA.) Note the influence the stress placement, shown by / ˈ/, on the second syllable has on the first vowel in /səˈmænθə/. You'll be in a better position to correct your versions once you've read the next chapter.

If you want to find out more:

Crystal, D. (2005) *How Language Works.* London: Penguin.

Chapter 9, 'How we describe speech sounds', includes a brief rationale of the IPA (pp.53–56).

Bloomer, A., Griffiths, P. and Merrison, A.J. (2005) *Introducing Language in Use. A coursebook.* London: Routledge.

This has an explanation of how the IPA system is organised (pp.252–4).

You can find the entire chart of IPA symbols (of which English uses a small sub-set) in Cruttenden, A. (2001) *Gimson's pronunciation of English 6th ed.* London: Arnold, p.3; in Roach, P. (2000) *English Phonetics and Phonology. A practical course* (3rd ed). Cambridge: Cambridge University Press, p.xi; and in Bloomer *et al.* (2005) as above, p.492.

Answer to Task 1

16 symbols are used with familiar consonantal sound values: /p,b,t,d,k,g,f,v,m,n,s, z,h,w,r,l/

Chapter 4
Phonetics – the basics

Phonetics is the study of speech sounds, and forms one branch of linguistics, the science of language. Textbooks on phonetics, and phonetics chapters within linguistics books, even the most basic, often look dauntingly technical and make too many assumptions about the knowledge base and interests of their readers. From many years of teaching phonetics to university students, and latterly to adult basic skills teachers, I have learnt that many phoneticians fail to appreciate that teaching it in a decontextualised, overly 'linguistic' way can be off-putting for non-specialists who are keen to know how to apply the knowledge rather than simply to enjoy it for its own sake – fascinating though it is.

I shall attempt to root this account firmly in practice, referring to the Adult Literacy Core Curriculum and a progression in phonics for reading and spelling. This chapter also lays a solid foundation by sharing some 'technical' terms and concepts, which will form a useful and necessary 'metalinguistic tool bag' (Bloomer *et al.*, 2005, p.9) for you to draw on.

In the introduction I mentioned both 'phonetics' and 'phonology'. Informally, the terms are often used interchangeably. They are distinct studies, but the distinction needn't greatly concern us, as there is considerable overlap in practice. In essence, the distinction is between, on the one hand, the actual sounds of a language and, on the other, how those sounds are organised in a given language. To describe how the sounds of English are produced by the vocal apparatus is a matter of phonetics; to describe the patterns made by these sounds – in other words, how the 44 phonemes of English are arranged in order to express meaning – is in the realm of phonology.

As noted earlier, a phoneme means a sound. But not all sounds in a given language are phonemes, as we shall see later. The identification of phonemes is based on identifying those sounds which cause a change in meaning. Thus, if we look at the initial sounds of the English words <big, pig, fig, gig>, each change of sound results in a change of meaning (and a 'different' word) so /b,p,f,g/ are all phonemes of English. This creation of 'minimal pairs' will also work with the final consonant sound, e.g. <big, bit, bitch, bin, bill, bib, bid>. Now we will try focusing on the vowel sound:

Task 2

Using <big> as the starting point, see how many different vowel phonemes you can identify by forming minimal pairs.

(Answers at the end of the chapter)

(You will observe that not every phoneme can be used in every position to make a meaningful word, so for example there are no words *<bim> /bɪm/ or *<beeg> /biːg/(but you can, of course, get <him> /hɪm/ and <league>/liːg/). Note that an asterisk preceding a potential word is the convention for indicating that it does not occur.)

Phonemes can be divided into vowels and consonants; for English, most accents have around 20 vowel phonemes and 24 consonant phonemes. The distinction is a familiar one and can be explained on both phonetic and phonological grounds, which I won't explore in detail here, other than to note the following:

- The sounds produced depend on different positions of the speech organs (tongue, lips, etc.). With consonants, there is an obstruction to the air flow, either complete or partial. For example, in the /p/ sound the lips come together and block the flow of air completely (a 'bilabial' or two-lip sound). But /f/ is different: contact is between the bottom lip and the teeth (a 'labiodental' or lip-tongue sound), and enough air comes through to make it possible to achieve a long drawn out /ffffff.../ sound. Try that with /p/ and it is simply not possible. If you imagine you can, what you will be producing is actually /p/ followed by a vowel sound, e.g. 'puu.....h'. (This is a feature with implications for the 'sounding out' that phonics involves, discussed in the next chapter.) By contrast, there is no obstruction in the vocal tract when vowel sounds are produced, so the sound can be prolonged until you run out of breath – 'aaaaaah'...!
- Another way of distinguishing vowels from consonants is one that is instinctive for native speakers of English: we say '**a** banana' but '**an** apple', i.e. two different forms of the indefinite article precede consonants and vowels respectively. The distinction is also there in the use of the definite article, although this time it is not reflected in the spelling: say 'the banana' and 'the apple' and you will find that the first sounds like /ðə/ and the second like /ðiː/. (Refer back to the IPA list for these characters.)
- An accurate understanding of the vowel and consonant inventory of English is vital for effective delivery of phonics. Anything less has the potential to mislead your learners. It is not necessary to memorise all the different phonetic terms to describe the phonemes of English, but an awareness of how and where in the vocal tract they are produced will be helpful to you and your learners. Careful listening

and 'testing' out on yourself, noting the positions of tongue and lips, will be invaluable.

Consonants

Consonant sounds are relatively straightforward, and familiarising yourself with the IPA list will probably suffice. There is less variation between accents in consonants than in vowels. Phonetics books usually list the consonants according to their **manner of articulation**, further subdivided into **place of articulation**. Such detail is not required here, although further reading is suggested at the end of this chapter for those who wish to pursue this further. 'Articulation' is concerned with how the vocal organs (larynx, tongue, teeth, lips, etc.) affect the airstream to produce the different sounds. Certainly an awareness of where in the mouth sounds are produced (place of articulation) is useful, if only to help learners with various sounds; e.g. pointing out the difference between /m/ and /n/ could be demonstrated as the difference between closing both lips for /m/ ('bilabial') and keeping the lips slightly apart and the tongue tip on the ridge behind the top teeth ('alveolar') for /n/.

'Manner of articulation' deals with how the air escapes from the closure in the vocal tract, whether there is a complete closure as for /p,b, t,d, k,g/, which are known as 'stops' or 'plosives', or partial closure as for /f,v, θ,ð, s,z, ʃ,ʒ, h/ which are 'fricatives', where the speech organs are close enough for the escaping air to produce a hissing noise or friction.

Many of the consonant phonemes come in related pairs, /p,b; t,d; k,g; f,v; s,z; θ,ð; ʃ,ʒ/. The distinction is called '**voicing**', whereby the vocal cords in the larynx vibrate ('voiced' sounds) or not ('voiceless' sounds). Try this out with /f/ and /v/ by placing your hand on your Adam's apple while you say these two sounds. You should feel a vibration for /v/ – it is the voiced member of the pair – but not for /f/. Why is voicing important? You are probably aware that the distinction between voiced and voiceless members of such pairs is not always reflected in the spelling. Let's illustrate this with the words <cats> and <dogs>. Both end in grapheme <s>; the sound at the end of <cats> is /s/ but at the end of <dogs> it's /z/. Why is this? Try saying them the other way round 'catz' and 'dogss' – it's very awkward. It is because of a process called 'assimilation', which means that adjacent sounds change to be more like one another and easier to pronounce. Thus, if you have a voiceless consonant it's easier to follow it with another voiceless one, and similarly for voiced consonants. This phenomenon means that consonant clusters – adjacent consonant phonemes – in English are either all voiced or all voiceless.

Task 3

Ignoring the spelling, try saying the words <husband> <cooked> <Asda> <Tesco> <leaves> <rushed> <next>. In each case note the consonant cluster created and where the voicing is not reflected in the spelling.

(Answers at the end of the chapter.)

Other consonants, which are not in voiceless/voiced pairs, tend to be voiced. If you say words such as <Sainsbury> <pulled> <limbs>, you will hear the clusters as, respectively, /nzb/, /ld/ and /mz/. What happens with <x> in words such as <exit> or <examine>? Do you say /ˈeksɪt/ or /ˈegzɪt/? Either is possible, but not */ˈegsɪt/ or */ˈekzɪt/.

Another type of assimilation concerns place of articulation and happens commonly with the nasal consonants /m, n, ŋ/. Say the words, <bump>, <hunt> and note that /m, p/ are both bilabial consonants (made with the lips together), and /n, t/ are both 'alveolar' (with the tongue on the bony ridge behind the upper front teeth). /ŋ/ is a 'velar' nasal, whereby the back of the tongue is raised against the back of the mouth (the velum, or soft palate). If you say the words <finger> <thank> <ink> <include>, in each case there is a velar consonant /k/ or /g/ immediately following the velar nasal. (Note here that the phoneme /ŋ/ is not necessarily represented by the grapheme <ng>; in each of these words the correspondence is with <n>, not <ng>.) All that is happening is that the pronunciation is made easier by having both sounds produced in the same part of the mouth. Try saying <*bunp> or <*humt> or <fin-ger> (*/ˈfɪngə/) and there is more effort involved in the process of changing where the sound is made. Above all, the phenomenon of assimilation illustrates that consonant phonemes cannot be fully understood in isolation; it is their behaviour in words that matters. Meaningful phonics teaching focuses not just on isolated phonemes but on strings of phonemes in words.

Vowels

Not only are there more unfamiliar IPA symbols to learn for vowel phonemes, but vowels are harder to pinpoint and describe, with great individual and regional variation possible. There is no exact place of articulation using tongue, teeth and lips as for consonants. Phonetics textbooks contain elaborate diagrams of the positions of the vowels, but here it will be sufficient to note the following:

- There are articulation clues in the shape of the mouth when pronouncing vowels. See and feel the difference, for example, when you say /iː aː uː/ (‘ee’, ‘ah’, ‘oo’).

- Vowels can be divided into ‘short’, ‘long’ and ‘diphthongs’. Long vowels are indicated by length marks /ː/. The two additional vowel phonemes listed in the IPA chart from the Core Curriculum in Appendix 2 (/i, u/) have been created by adding two of the long vowels, minus their length marks. These do reflect the way the vowels in certain words are pronounced, but it would be difficult to find minimal pairs to ‘prove’ that they are actually phonemes, i.e. distinctive sounds that make a difference of meaning. Often what are referred to informally as ‘long vowels’ are in fact diphthongs, which involve a glide from one sound to another and are transcribed using two IPA symbols; try saying /eɪ / (as in <eight>) and /aʊ / (as in <out>) and feel the shape of your mouth change. Rather misleadingly, the letters <a, e, i, o, u>, to distinguish them from their short versions /æ, e, ɪ, ɒ, ʌ/, are often described as ‘saying their names’ when long. Only one of these ‘letter-name vowels’ is actually a straightforward long vowel. One is a long vowel preceded by a consonant, the others are diphthongs.

Task 4

Try transcribing each of the letter-name vowels, and identifying which phoneme(s) each contains.

(Answers at the end of the chapter.)

As with consonants, it is how vowels behave in words that is especially important. For vowels, we need to pay attention to word stress, by which we mean the degree of force or emphasis with which a syllable is spoken. (Be aware that some phonetics books refer to this force as ‘accent’, but this term is best avoided; ‘accent’ is the usual term to describe features of pronunciation, see Chapter 7.) In phonetic transcription, a stressed syllable is indicated by the mark /'/ immediately preceding the syllable, e.g. <polite>/pə'laɪt/. In particular, we need to distinguish between stressed syllables and unstressed syllables in order to understand the vowel phoneme /ə/, known as 'schwa' and written like a rotated <e>. Except when it forms the second element in the three diphthongs /eə, ɪə, ʊə/, schwa can usually only occur in unstressed syllables. It can be spelled using any of the vowel graphemes, although <a> is its most frequent spelling. However, don't be tempted to assume that all vowels in unstressed syllables are schwa. Many are, but the unstressed first vowel in <immense>, /ɪ'mens/, for example, is not.

Task 5

Try identifying the schwa vowels in the following words; read them at normal conversational speed, and see how many different graphemes you can find to represent schwa. You should start by noting the stressed syllables first. (Note that graphemes of more than one letter may be involved, and some words may have more than one schwa vowel.):

<farmer, about, colour, figure, famous, oblige, doctor, suppose, gentlemen, exam>

(Answers at the end of the chapter.)

There are another couple of stress-related points we need to keep in mind about vowels:

- Stress shifts can affect vowel phonemes, even when the graphemes remain the same, e.g. in word pairs such as <present> /'prezənt/ (noun) and /prɪ'zent/(verb); conduct /'kɒndʌkt/ (noun) and /

kən'dʌkt/ (verb); and the alternative pronunciations of <research> /rɪ'sɜːʧ/ and /'riːsɜːʧ/.

- Vowel phonemes can disappear altogether immediately before or immediately after a stressed syllable, e.g. <raspberry>. In normal speech we don't actually say /'rɑːspberiː/ but something closer to /'rɑːzbriː/. This illustrates two separate phenomena – 1) the disappearance or 'elision' of the vowel sound immediately after the stressed first syllable; 2) 'assimilation' such that the consonants in the cluster share the same voicing, i.e. /z, b/.

Before leaving our discussion of vowels and in the hope of reassuring readers, who may be worried about the complexity of vowel phonemes, it is worth pointing out that it tends to be consonants which actually carry the information in words (e.g. f u cn rd ths thn wats th prblm?) and this is the very feature, of course, that is exploited in texting (Crystal, 2008). We will look at some of the implications of these new forms of written language in Chapters 6 and 7.

So far we have been looking at phonemes and how they behave in words. In purely phonetic terms, the situation is actually more complex. We are concerned primarily with differences of sounds that are meaningful, i.e. make a difference of meaning. However, if you listen very carefully, you will hear subtler distinctions such as the quality of the /l/ sounds in a word such as <lull> where, in RP at least, the initial /l/ can be described as 'clear' and the final /l/ as 'dark'. Say the word and note that the tongue position is slightly different – the tip moves further back in the mouth for the final /l/. (Try reversing the sounds, to start with a dark /l/ and finish with a clear /l/ – it feels and sounds rather odd.) It seems that literate people become 'conditioned' to stop hearing differences in the quality of the /l/ since both are represented by grapheme <l> (and the meaning is not affected).

Similarly the 'voiceless plosives' /p, t, k/ can change how they sound depending on where they occur in a word (or syllable). Compare the following words: <pin, nip, spin, bin> /pɪn, nɪp, spɪn, bɪn/. Say them aloud, holding the back of your hand in front of your mouth. You should feel a definite puff of air ('aspiration') accompanying the /p/ in <pin>, which is rather less in word-final position in <nip>, and disappears when /s/ precedes /p/ in <spin>. The voiced one of the pair, /b/, carries no aspiration. The main way we distinguish between /p/ and /b/ is actually in the presence or absence of aspiration. There are many such cases of variants of phonemes being in 'complementary distribution', i.e. they can be predicted depending on where they occur in a word. Furthermore, sometimes the sound of a consonant can be affected by which vowel follows it, e.g. in the words <keep, cart> the initial /k/ is articulated differently (the mouth shapes differ) in anticipation of the following vowel - front vowel /iː/ in /kiːp/ versus back vowel /ɑː/ in kɑːt/. These variations on phonemes are known as 'allophones' and do not affect the meaning of words in English. Thus, they do not directly concern the delivery of phonics; however, the phonics teacher needs to be aware of them, especially as sharp-eared learners may pick up some of these differences and interpret them as having different phoneme-grapheme correspondences.

We now need to look at what happens in connected speech. What we have been dealing with so far are individual words or 'citation forms'. Further changes can occur with sequences of words, and the faster the speech, the more changes there can be. For example, take the phrase <bread and butter>. Only if it is said very slowly does the word <and> sound like /ænd/; usually the phrase is pronounced /'bred ən 'bʌtə/ - this is not 'careless' speech, merely normal conversational usage. Not only has /æ/ been reduced to /ə/, being unstressed, but the three-consonant cluster created across the word boundary between <and> and <butter> /ndb/ has been reduced to /nb/, with the elision of the middle consonant /d/. This is very common across word boundaries; think about the phrases <next day, first night, must do>, plus of course lots of other 'and' phrases. The change of /æ/ to schwa in <and> also illustrates what happens to many other 'function words' (pronouns, conjunctions, prepositions, etc.) in connected speech: when unstressed, their 'weak' forms are used, whereby whatever vowel phoneme might feature in a citation form, it usually becomes a schwa, e.g. <from, to, at, but, can, than>, etc.

Task 6

Read the following sentence out very slowly and then speed up to normal conversational speed:

<I'm happy to stay at home from day to day for now, but can see myself getting even more bored than you do.>

Transcribe this, noting all the function words that would become weak forms here.

(Answers at the end of the chapter.)

You can find useful lists of weak forms to refer to in, for example, Cruttenden (2001, pp.252–3) and Roach (2000, pp.114–20).

There are other interesting connected speech phenomena which you can read about in textbooks such as Cruttenden (2001, pp.249–95) and Roach (2000, pp.134–49). Space does not permit discussion of them all, although **linking /r/** and **intrusive /r/** are worth a brief mention. We are aware that in many accents of English, including RP, when there is an <r> in the written version of a word, it is only pronounced

/r/ before vowels, and not in syllable-final position, e.g. <remember> is pronounced /rɪ'membə/. However, in the phrase <remember it>, there is a 'linking' /r/ because the second word <it> begins with a vowel and thus the second <r> now precedes a vowel across the word boundary to produce /rɪ'membər ɪt/. 'Intrusive /r/' occurs to link one word which ends in a vowel with the next one if it also begins with a vowel, even when there is no <r> in the spelling, e.g. <media event> is frequently pronounced /'miːdiər ɪ'vent/; <law and order> becomes the notorious 'Laura Norder' (which also serves to illustrate the common reduction, already discussed, of /ænd/ to /ən/.

Remember, above all, that connected speech is how your adult learners will be accustomed to speaking and listening. The ability to isolate citation forms is a function of literacy. Careful listening at all times is important, so you are alert to the variations that occur naturally in different types of speech and in different contexts. Further variations in how phonemes are pronounced also occur with different regional and national accents, and are the topic of Chapter 7.

Finally, since the aim of this introduction to phonetics and phonology is to equip you to help your learners become better readers and spellers, I shall close with an exercise that directly links phonetics with literacy. The topic is one I call 'deliberately deviant spelling'. You are aware, especially in advertising, that wrong spellings are used as eye-catching marketing devices – brand names such as 'Kwik-fit, Kleeneze, Blu Tack', etc. To be effective they must involve unambiguous grapheme-phoneme correspondences. If they don't, they don't work. Many years ago there was a type of shampoo for blondes called 'Stā-blond'. As a child, I pronounced it /'staːblɒnd/ ('Star-blonde'), failing to appreciate that /'steɪblɒnd/ ('stay blonde') was presumably what was intended!

Task 7

Have a look round for deliberate misspellings – brand names, businesses, shop names (hairdressers and fast food outlets can be a rich hunting ground) and work out if they are successful or not in terms of their correspondences. Some, of course, rely more on visual effect, e.g. the chain of 'Rɘvolution' bars.

If you want to find out more:

There are numerous textbooks on English phonetics and phonology, some of which have far more detail than you will need. One of the clearest, however, is:

Roach, P. (2000) *English Phonetics and Phonology. A practical course* (3rd Edition) Cambridge: Cambridge University Press.

This is aimed at university students and 'practising English language teachers'.

Cruttenden, A. (2001) *Gimson's pronunciation of English* (6th Edition) London: Arnold.

This is an update of a classic in its field, and is excellent for reference purposes; each consonant and vowel phoneme is listed, with examples of how it is represented by different spellings.

For briefer introductory chapters on phonetics within general linguistics books, you could try:

Bloomer, A., Griffiths, P. and Merrison, A. J. (2005) *Introducing Language in Use. A coursebook.* London: Routledge, Chapter 8 *Phonetics,* pp.232–73;

Crystal, D. (2005) *How Language Works.* London: Penguin, pp.18–72; or

Graddol, D., Cheshire, J. and Swann, J. (1994)

Describing Language (2nd Edition) Buckingham: Open University Press, Chapter 2, *The sounds of language*, pp.28–58.

Answers to tasks

Task 2

Minimal pairs, based on <big> /bɪg/– <bag, beg, bog, bug, berg> five vowel phonemes – /æ, e, ɒ, ʌ, ɜː/.

(Don’t be misled into thinking there’s a /r/ sound in the last one.)

Task 3

/zb; kt; zd; sk; vz; ʃt; kst/

Task 4

<a> /eɪ/, <i> /aɪ/, <o> /əʊ/ – diphthongs

<e> /iː/ – pure long vowel

<u> /juː/ – long vowel preceded by consonant

Task 5

/'fɑːmə/ = <er>; /ə'baʊt/ = <a>; /'kʌlə/ = <our>; /'fɪgə/ = <ure>; /'feɪməs/ = <ou>; /ə'blaɪʤ/ = <o>; /'dɒktə/ = <or>; /sə'pəʊz/ = <u>; /'ʤentəlmən/ = <e>; /ɪg'zæm/ (no schwa here – just to remind you that not every unstressed vowel = schwa)

Task 6

Variations are possible here, depending on emphasis and speed of delivery, but one transcription might be:

/aɪm 'hæpiː tə steɪ ət 'həʊm frəm deɪ tə deɪ fə 'naʊ bət kən 'siː mə'self getɪŋ 'iːvən mɔː 'bɔːd ðən 'juː duː/

Don’t be tempted to reduce every unstressed vowel phoneme to schwa.

Chapter 5

Spelling and the Core Curriculum: Progression in phonics

Now that we are armed with the basics of the phonetics and phonology of English, and have some familiarity with the IPA transcription system, I would next like to consider how this underpinning knowledge can support the delivery of phonics in the classroom. As already mentioned, this is not a book on how to teach phonics as such, but it is important to relate phonetic knowledge to the planning and delivery of a progression in phonics.

Rather than single out any particular phonics scheme or framework as the structure for this chapter, I shall take the requirements of the Adult Literacy Core Curriculum, accessed online at: **www.excellencegateway.org.uk/sflcurriculum**, as my starting point for a discussion of some of the issues involved.

However the relationship between reading and writing is viewed, it is good practice to use writing to reinforce reading, and vice versa. We shall start by looking at the Core Curriculum's guidelines for writing, although there are places where it seems that phonics for reading and phonics for spelling are not always clearly distinguished. A phonics approach for spelling was a strategy used by teachers in the Phonics Project with learners up to Level 2.

Entry level 1

Ww E1.3 ***Use basic sound symbol association to help spelling as appropriate for the needs of the learner.***

Some important points are made:

- *Understand that sounds are associated with letters and strings of letters.*
- *Understand that there are more sounds (phonemes) than letters of the alphabet, so some sounds are represented by combinations of letters.*
- *Know how to identify and segment phonemes in words for spelling, and understand that decoding for reading is the reverse operation of encoding for spelling.*

The last two points require some expansion. While there are certainly more sounds (44) than letters (26), the total number of graphemes in English spelling is at least 238 (Mountford, 1998, p.113). This means that the statement that decoding and encoding are 'reverse' operations, although true in one sense, rather oversimplifies the position. Encoding for spelling is far more complex than decoding for reading, as there are many more correspondence possibilities and because the 'rules' are not necessarily reversible.

'***Activities and examples'*** in this section of the Curriculum include:

> *'Hear identify and write initial and final phonemes and short medial vowel sounds in consonant-vowel-consonant words; hear and segment initial consonant clusters and final consonant clusters; hear identify and write consonant digraphs.'*

There is a lot for the learner to take on board here, even when dealing with one-syllable words.

- **Consonants**: Some consonant phonemes are more regularly spelt than others; the less regular phonemes may have to be analysed according to their position in a word (e.g. /f/ is <f> initially, but often <ff> word-finally, not to mention <ph>).

  In all positions /b d g h m n p r t θ ð/ are regularly <b d g h m n p r t th th>.

  /w/ does not occur in final position. Word-initially and medially it is represented as <w> (although medially only in compound words such as 'upwards'). It behaves differently in certain clusters, as explained in the next bullet point.

  /ŋ/ does not occur initially and is regularly spelt <n> before /k/ and /g/ (e.g. <sink, finger>), otherwise <ng> (e.g. <thing, hanger>). For the other consonant phonemes, refer to the checklist of correspondences in Appendix 3.

- The difficulties that some learners have with hearing the different phonemes in **consonant clusters** will be discussed in the next chapter. There are also some peculiarities of spelling to contend with, e.g. clusters where the second element is /w/ are spelt with <u> after /k/ and sometimes after /s/ and /g/, e.g. <quick, squirrel, suite, language>, otherwise <w>, e.g <swim, twin>; the assimilation of voicing, discussed in Chapter 4, means that in final clusters /z/ is written <s> when it is the marker for plural, possessive or present tense, as in <dogs, Rob's, hides>, etc.

- **Short medial vowel sounds** do form a good starting point as they are relatively 'regular'. Two of them, /æ, e/, have regular spellings as <a, e> wherever they occur (the notable exception being the 'head, bread' series where /e/ = <ea>). Each of the other short vowels (except /ʊ/) has a predominant spelling, i.e. /ɪ, ɒ, ʌ, ə/ as <i, o, u, a>.

Ww E1.4 ***Develop a variety of strategies to aid spelling***

Note that some of the visual strategies are really only suitable for learners at later stages. The concept of something 'looking right', popular with some teachers, or of finding 'words inside words' might only make sense to someone who is already experienced enough with reading and/or secure enough in spelling. Perhaps a more helpful approach in the early stages might be the concept of a 'good mistake', where what is written, although wrong, involves a valid phoneme–grapheme correspondence, e.g. *<creem> for <cream>.

Entry level 2

Ww E2.2 ***Use their knowledge of sound-symbol relationships and phonological patterns (e.g. consonant clusters and vowel phonemes) to help work out correct spellings as appropriate for the needs of the learner***

To this end further points made include the following:

- *Understand that most irregular words have at least some regular elements.*

Even the most 'irregular' word will still have some 'clues' to its spelling in its phoneme–grapheme correspondences. This becomes tricky to deal with when the initial phoneme is hard to encode, so looking the word up in a dictionary is a less helpful option e.g. <one> (although /n/ is still represented as <ne>)

- *Understand that it is possible to greatly reduce the chances of making random spelling errors by applying their knowledge of spelling patterns and rules.*

Spelling 'rules' need to be treated with caution as they

are by no means foolproof. As Masha Bell says in her helpful spelling primer, 'The hardest part of learning to spell English is memorising all the exceptions to basic spelling rules, rather than the rules themselves' (Bell, 2009, p.4).

Entry level 3

Ww E3.2 ***Use their developing knowledge of sound-symbol relationships and phonological patterns to help spell a greater range of words and longer words, as appropriate for the needs of the learner***

- *Understand that there is not always a strict sound-symbol association in spelling, e.g. silent letters.*

This is rather a misleading statement. There is always a sound-symbol association involved! If there weren't, then spelling really would be random. Also, the concept of 'silent letters' is best avoided as unhelpful. Far better is an approach that says, for example, 'The /n/ sound at the beginning of /naɪf/ (<knife>) is spelt <kn>', articulated as 'kay, en' using the letter names to emphasise that here the letters do not have separate phonemic values. Although it is essential to use the 'phonemic alphabet' when dealing with simple spellings involving one-to-one correspondences between phonemes and letters, letter names become indispensable as soon as learners encounter the first digraph (two-letter grapheme), e.g. <kn>. This approach also recognises that phonemes can be represented in different ways, including by graphemes that also happen to be associated with other phonemes. <igh> is a trigraph (three-letter grapheme) spelling phoneme /aɪ/ as a unit, and does not have 'silent' <g> and <h> (or worse, silent /g/ and /h/!). <igh> is one of four common ways of representing phoneme /aɪ/, along with <i.e.>, <y> and (in non-final syllables in words of more than one syllable) <i> on its own, e.g. <light, bite, my, pilot>. As one phonics learner said, 'When I've seen words with <igh> in, I've not been able to work them out. Now I know... that there's only one sound' (Burton, 2007, p.12).

- *Understand that segmenting words into phonemes and breaking them into syllables (beats) and components (compounds) helps work out spelling.*

Reservations about syllables will be mentioned again in the next chapter under Rw E2.2. Are they helpful for spelling? Breaking words into syllables would not necessarily by itself address the problems of encoding unstressed vowels, unless note is actually taken of where the stress falls, e.g. a learner faced with spelling /tə'deɪ/ would probably find the spelling of the second syllable straightforward – the familiar word <day> – but might be less certain over several possibilities for spelling the schwa vowel in the first syllable since <a> is more frequent for this in general than the correct <o> in this word.

As this is not intended to be a spelling primer, I shall finish here by referring you again to the tables in Appendix 3, which you can use to cross-check some of the more common spelling possibilities.

If you want to find out more:

Bell, M. (2009) *Rules and Exceptions of English Spelling.* Cambridge: Pegasus Educational – a clear, helpful and linguistically sound booklet.

Chapter 6

Reading and the Core Curriculum: progression in phonics

There is no mention of phonics as such at **pre-Entry** level, although there is a requirement (Rw/M8.2) to 'associate sounds with patterns in some letters, syllables, words, rhymes and songs', in other words phonological awareness is to be encouraged. For many adults who are competent users of spoken language, this is a stage that would probably not be required.

Entry level 1

Rw E1.2 ***Decode simple regular words***

It is perhaps symptomatic of the ambivalent reception still accorded to phonics that prediction of sense and meaning through context and 'own language experience' are suggested as strategies *before* decoding through recognition of correspondences between letters and sounds. Research evidence shows that phonics should really be the first port of call; useful as prediction strategies can be, of course, they do not equip the learner to decode other, unfamiliar words.

To quote the Core Curriculum:

- *Understand that written words correspond to their spoken equivalents and are composed of letters in combinations to represent spoken sounds.*
- *Identify sounds in familiar regular words from spoken experience and recognise correspondence between sounds (phonemes) and letters (graphemes).*

Certainly recognition of the basic relationship between the letters on the page and the sounds of speech is a crucial element, and 'regular' words are a good route to the understanding of that relationship. Unfortunately some of the commonest and most 'familiar' words have rather less regular correspondences, e.g. <to, the, no, go, I, into> (all words which the *Letters and Sounds* framework suggests can be introduced to learners at the very start of phonics instruction). It is also worth noting that words that seem hard at the start become easier to decode once further correspondences have been learnt. (For a full list of the high-frequency words that *Letters and Sounds* suggests as sight vocabulary, see Burton *et al.*, 2008, p.47.)

The Entry level 1 ***'activities and examples'*** include recognition of correspondences in *'initial consonant letter sounds, short vowel sounds, initial consonant clusters and final consonant clusters'*. There are a lot of correspondences to learn and it would be important to build them up a few at a time, with frequent revision. Many phonics teachers would recommend leaving consonant clusters (defined as two adjacent consonant phonemes, such as /sp, tr, fl/, etc.) until later on; certainly teachers have found that in the early stages some learners struggle with clusters, finding it hard to blend two consonant phonemes together. Some schemes, including *Letters and Sounds,* actually recommend introducing the most common consonant digraphs (two graphemes, one phoneme, e.g. <ch, sh, th, ng>) before consonant clusters. Many of these have regular correspondences. Note that the single grapheme <x>, of course, usually represents the consonant clusters /ks/ or /gz/ (as in <axe, exact>, /æks, ɪgˈzækt/). It is important to be very clear about how many phonemes are involved and resist the temptation to find one-to-one correspondences where they do not exist.

Two final points I would like to add:

- The extent to which you share the metalinguistic vocabulary of 'phonemes', 'graphemes', etc. with your learners very much depends on your learners. These terms are in use in primary school literacy classes, so parents might welcome knowing them. Furthermore, some teachers find the sharing of such terminology 'empowering' for the learners (Burton, 2008, p.20).
- 'Sounding out' can be a minefield. Be particularly careful with the 'plosive' consonants (/p,b; t,d; k,g/ plus nasals /n, m/). As mentioned in Chapter 4, plosives involve a complete closure in the mouth, preventing air from escaping. They can be sounded out only if accompanied by a vowel sound and the danger lies in putting too much emphasis on the vowel. Sounding out is the preparatory stage to blending the sounds together into words, and this is made far harder if the learner recites, e.g., 'duuh-o-guuh' and is expected to blend these sounds into /dɒg/ (<dog>). Keep the accompanying vowel sound minimal, like a very short schwa. Also be aware of the influence of consonant letter names where the vowel sound precedes the consonant sound(s), as in <f, l, m, n, s, x>, and can interfere with the learner's attempts to blend. Resist saying, for example, 'el' rather than the more helpful /lə/. (Also note that in letter name <r>, although there is actually no consonant phoneme sound /r/ when in isolation, in the alphabetic sequence <r, s>, a /r/ is sounded, thanks to the phenomenon of 'linking /r/' mentioned in Chapter 4). The influence of certain texting conventions does not help here, with their deliberate exploitation of the letter-name values, e.g. 'ruok' for 'are you okay?'

Entry level 2

Rw E2.2 ***Use context cues and own knowledge and experience to predict unknown words***

Again the emphasis seems to be on strategies to be used prior to phonics for decoding purposes, although this section also provides commentary on the next stages of phonics. A couple of points from the Curriculum merit further discussion:

- *Understand that the same sound (phoneme) can be spelt in more than one way and the same spelling (grapheme) can represent more than one sound.*

Indeed, with many more graphemes than phonemes, the range of possibilities is even greater in the phoneme-grapheme direction than the grapheme-phoneme direction, as mentioned in the previous chapter.

- *Understand how each beat in a word is a syllable – breaking some words into syllables can help to decode them.*

In my experience syllable division does not often seem to help learners to decode; syllable boundaries are not always straightforward, e.g. the word <extra> contains three different possibilities according to the laws of phonotactics (what sounds can be combined in syllables) – /ek-strə/, /eks-trə/, or /ekst-rə/ (but not /*ekstr-ə/ or /*e-kstrə/). However, the number of syllables in a word is rarely contested and the exercise of beating out syllables to distinguish stressed from unstressed syllables would usefully accompany the introduction of the vowel phonemes found in unstressed syllables, notably schwa /ə/.

The ***'activities and examples'*** include *'read words with common spelling patterns for long vowel phonemes'.*

Illustrations are given of the vowel sounds with their

different phoneme-grapheme correspondences. No distinction is made between long vowels and diphthongs as they are all grouped under 'long vowels'. Note that there are single long vowel sounds with basic two-grapheme correspondences, e.g. iː – <ee> as in <sleep> and (more unusually) diphthongs with basic one-grapheme correspondences, e.g. /əʊ/ – <o> as in <go>. However, most of the correspondences for short vowels involve a single grapheme. (For a useful checklist of 'basic' and 'other' correspondences for vowels, see Appendix 3.)

Entry level 3

Rw E3.5 Here the emphasis is on '*a variety of reading strategies to help decode an increasing range of unfamiliar words*'. Under the heading of '***activities and examples'*** it suggests '*read common words with silent letters (knife, wrist, etc.)*. The use of the term 'silent letter' is very widespread but, as explained in the previous chapter, may not be the most helpful way of characterising such correspondences. It is better to say that (in order of frequency) <n, nn, kn> can all represent /n/, and <r, rr, wr> can all represent /r/, and so on. It is interesting to note that when there is a doubled consonant grapheme, there is only one consonant sound (unlike languages such as Finnish and Italian), but we never seem to refer to the 'spare' letter as 'silent'. One learner is reported as saying that she hadn't realised before that when the same two letters come together (e.g. <nn> in 'dinner') there's only one sound (Burton, 2007, p.27).

What tends to happen when teaching phonics is that, once the learner has grasped the basic correspondences, and the principles of sounding out and blending, this knowledge will generate an understanding of other correspondences. It is not necessary to teach every single possible correspondence to enable a learner to become a competent reader. (Mountford, 1998, identified 407 phoneme–grapheme correspondences, far too many to teach or learn explicitly.)

A summarised progression, based on *Letters and Sounds,* can be found in Burton *et al.* (2008, pp.46–47). Tables of phoneme–grapheme and grapheme–phoneme correspondences of British English spelling are included for reference purposes in Appendix 3 in this book.

If you want to find out more:

Letters and Sounds, although aimed at primary school children, sets out a clear progression in phonics. This is a framework, rather than a 'scheme', so does not include materials. It is available free or downloadable from: **http://nationalstrategies.standards.dcsf.gov.uk/node/84969**

Chapter 7

Does accent matter? Issues of different varieties of language

One of the concerns that those practitioners who took part in the phonics project raised was how to cope with the variety of accents of English in which their learners operated. These could encompass not just British accents but other European, Asian, African and Caribbean varieties, even in non-ESOL classes. (Note that sometimes the word 'accent' is used in the sense of 'stress', meaning the prominent part of a word, as discussed in Chapter 4; avoid this.) Here we refer to 'accents' as meaning features of pronunciation, as distinct from 'dialects', which involve language varieties distinguished by differences of vocabulary and grammar. The Standard English dialect (the 'educated' standard, used for more formal writing) can be spoken with a variety of accents, not just received pronunciation (RP) – and usually is, as RP speakers form only a small minority of English speakers; however, regional or other national dialects of English are usually associated with the corresponding accent. Thus, someone saying 'wee bairn' to refer to a little child would be far more likely to pronounce the words in a Scottish or Tyneside accent than RP. (Try it!)

First, I would like to consider accent from a sociolinguistic point of view – that is, how language reflects the society in which it operates. Everyone speaks with an accent of one sort or another; even RP is just one of many accents of English. Informally, people don't tend to hear that they and their family/peers 'have an accent'. Thus, when we move to a different part of the country, the local accent may strike us initially; after a time we stop noticing it as much, as it becomes the default background accent, and our own accent may even acquire features of the new accent.

Accents give us important information about the identity of the speaker, both geographical and social. Much has been written about the relative status or 'prestige' of different accents, often with lists of which accents are thought to be the most 'acceptable' or 'trustworthy'. These are not necessarily topped by RP. Some Scottish accents are well regarded (and hence advertising favourites), with some urban accents being (apparently) mistrusted. These are very much subjective judgements, and adjectives such as 'harsh', 'rustic' or 'posh' would be meaningless in purely linguistic descriptions.

Task 8

Listen to a selection of advertisements on TV; note the types of accent being used and the effects they are trying to achieve.

Less contentious ground can be found in identifying accents solely by their geographical, rather than social, features, and dialectology is a fascinating study in its own right. There are many excellent books on this (see the end of this chapter for further reading suggestions) with maps showing lines (isoglosses) demarcating the geographical extent of different features. The online speech accent archive at **http://accent.gmu.edu**, mentioned earlier in Chapter 2, is also a fascinating resource. Here is a brief summary of some of the main features of British accents, contrasted with RP as a reference point:

RP	Variant	Location	Example	RP	Variant
/ʌ/	/ʊ/	North of line from the Severn to the Wash	<cup>	/kʌp/	/kʊp/
/ɑː/	/æ/	As above	<bath>	/bɑːθ/	/bæθ/
/ɔː/	/ɒ/	Scotland	<caught>	/kɔːt/	/kɒt/
/uː/	/ʊ/	Scotland	<pool>	/puːl/	/pʊl/
(non-rhotic)	/r/ (post-vocalic)	Scotland and West Country	<car>	/kɑː/	/kɑːr/ or /kær/
/juː/	/uː/	East Midlands and East Anglia	<beautiful>	/ˈbjuːtɪfʊl/	/ˈbuːtɪfʊl/ (the 'bootiful' of a certain Norfolk poultry producer!)

This is an oversimplification as, for instance, there are urban 'islands' within these broad areas which behave differently from surrounding areas. For example, there is no distinction in Liverpool between <fair> and <fir>, both tending to sound similar to /fɜː/; in Birmingham and the West Midlands, RP /aɪ/ becomes similar to /ɔɪ/, so <buy> sounds like /bɔɪ/ (<boy>); in London and, increasingly, in the South-East (so-called 'Estuary English'), /eɪ/ sounds more like /aɪ/ (e.g. the word <main> becomes /maɪn/); central Lancashire, including Oldham, uniquely for the North of England, has a rhotic accent (i.e. /r/ is pronounced after vowels where there is <r> in the spelling), e.g. <river> is pronounced as /ˈrɪvər/. This would be pronounced as /ˈrɪvə/ in RP which is 'non-rhotic', where /r/ is pronounced only before vowels, including across word boundaries (linking /r/).

What are the implications for phonics teaching? It can be noted that most of the variation affects vowels, which are generally more complicated, as we have already seen. Consonant variation can also be involved, as with post-vocalic /r/ in rhotic accents (above); the London Cockney and Estuary replacement of final /l/ with /ʊ / as in <hill> /hɪʊ/ and use of the glottal stop; and one of our teachers noted that a Caribbean learner tended to pronounce <th> as /t/ or /d/ (which can also be a feature of London Cockney in initial position, e.g. <the> as /də/; cf. the more usual loss of contrast between /f, θ/ and /v, ð/, which would produce <Cathy> as /'kæfiː/, and <together> as /tə'gevə/). But generally, consonants are more consistent across different accents, and this is noticeable in the language of the Internet and mobile phones ('netspeak'), where users harness what David Crystal refers to as 'the information value of consonants as opposed to vowels', to produce forms such as 'txt' and 'thx' where vowels are omitted, or 'ttyl' and 'lol' where only initial letters of words are used (Crystal, 2001, pp.229–30). We also mentioned in the previous chapter possible implications of this new type of written language for 'sounding out' in phonics.

It is important to remember that you are not there to give your learners elocution lessons (unless intelligibility is involved), although awareness of the structures and vocabulary of Standard English does need to be encouraged, at least for writing. Non-judgmental discussion of the relationships between different types of accents and dialects is the way forward. It is very important not to suggest that any particular accent is inferior. A link from the Core Curriculum reminds us:

- *All languages and their varieties have equal linguistic status.*
- *Language and identity are closely linked. Implied criticism of their primary variety of language can be alienating for learners.*

- *Learners who use some regional or social varieties of English may have low self-esteem because of this.*

(From *Standard English and other varieties of English*; link accessed from Rw L1.3)

This third point was brought home to me years ago, when I was teaching in the north of England, and had a Glaswegian learner in my class. He was convinced that his problems with reading and spelling stemmed from his Scottish accent! My attempts to persuade him otherwise, and that his pronunciation of, e.g. <former> as / 'fɒrmər/ (rather than, as in most English varieties, /'fɔːmə/) was actually rather helpful in terms of phoneme-grapheme correspondences, unfortunately left him unconvinced; his view that his speech was inferior was too deeply engrained.

What must be emphasised here above all is that having learners with accents other than RP does not exclude the use of phonics. The following quote illustrates a typical misunderstanding: 'It is not helpful to persist in practising phonic distinctions if the learner finds it difficult to discriminate between them. For example, in a variety of English spoken in South-East London, *i* and *e* sound very similar as in *will* and *well* ' (Hughes and Schwab, 2010, pp.167-8). What this means is that the distinction between phonemes /ɪ / and /e/ is lost in certain contexts, and in these the graphemes <i> and <e> can both correspond to phoneme /ɪ /. Indeed, on closer investigation of London English, the situation turns out to be even more interesting: it seems that /æ/ as in <sat> is becoming closer to the phoneme /e/, as well as /e/ in <set> being realised as /ɪ/, as mentioned above (Cruttenden, 2001, p.87). This complexity need not dismay the teacher of phonics. After all, even in RP, one-to-one vowel correspondences are in short supply. Thus, the grapheme-phoneme and phoneme-grapheme correspondences may well be different in different accents of English, but within each accent they can still be mapped out.

Task 9

To illustrate the above point, try listing the phonemes of a non-RP accent with which you are familiar, either your own or that of one of your learners, using the RP list in Appendix 1 as a guide. Then, using the spelling lists in Appendix 3 as a guide, map the phoneme-grapheme correspondences where they are different. For Northern English, for example, you will find:

Phoneme	**Grapheme(s)**	As in…
/æ/	<a>	and, ask
/ɑː/	<ar>	far

That is, you need to move <ask> from /ɑː/ to /æ/. From this you will also note that, although /æ/ replaces /ɑː/ in some contexts, the phoneme /aː/ still exists in Northern varieties of English, most often represented by grapheme <ar> (cf. Standard Scottish English where <ar> would be pronounced as /ær/, with the total loss of distinction made in RP between /æ/ and /ɑː/).

A final point to note is that languages are not static. All varieties, whether reflecting social or geographical differences, or influenced by new technologies, are subject to change over time. And these changes affect pronunciation as well as grammar and spelling. 'Prestige' accents are not resistant to change either: as you will have noticed, the RP accent heard in old black and white films or newsreels, or even in old TV programmes from only a few decades ago, is rather different from today's RP – which continues to evolve.

If you want to find out more:

Hughes, A., Trudgill, P. and Watt, D. (2005) *English Accents and Dialects. An Introduction to Social and Regional Varieties of British English*. London: Hodder.
This is a classic account, now into its 4th edition, and very readable, which covers a good range of geographical locations in Britain.

Cruttenden, A. (2001) *Gimson's Pronunciation of English*, 6th edition. London: Arnold.
Chapter 7 gives a detailed account of current changes within RP and describes characteristics of other accents of English, including Northern, Scottish, American and Australian.

Crystal, D. (1995) *The Cambridge Encyclopedia of the English language*. Cambridge: Cambridge University Press.

This deals entertainingly with regional and social variation in Chapters 20 and 21.

Crystal, D. (2008) *Txtng: The gr8 db8.* Oxford: Oxford University Press.

Provides an up-to-date and entertaining account of the linguistic features of texting.

References

Bell, M. (2009) *Rules and Exceptions of English Spelling.* Cambridge: Pegasus Educational.

Besser, S., Brooks, G., Burton, M., Parisella, M., Spare, Y., Stratford, S. and Wainwright, J. (2004) *Adult Literacy Learners' Difficulties in Reading: An exploratory study (research report).* London: National Research and Development Centre for Adult Literacy and Numeracy (NRDC).
Downloadable from: **www.nrdc.org.uk/publications_details.asp?ID=14**

Bloomer, A., Griffiths, P. and Merrison, A. J. (2005) *Introducing Language in Use. A coursebook.* London: Routledge.

Brooks, G., Burton, M., Cole, P. and Szczerbiński, M. (2007) *Effective Teaching and Learning: Reading.* London: NRDC.
Downloadable from: **www.nrdc.org.uk/publications_details.asp?ID=90**

Brunswick, N., McDougall, S. and de Mornay Davies, P. (eds) (2010) *Reading and Dyslexia in different orthographies.* Hove: Psychology Press.

Burton, M. (2007) *Reading. Developing adult teaching and learning: Practitioner Guide.* Leicester: NIACE.

Burton, M., Davey, J., Lewis, M., Ritchie, L. and Brooks, G. (2008) *Improving Reading: Phonics and fluency. Practitioner guide.* London: NRDC.
Downloadable from: **www.nrdc.org.uk/publications_details.asp?ID=156**

Burton, M., Davey, J., Lewis, M., Ritchie, L. and Brooks, G. (2010) *Progress for Adult Literacy Learners.* London: NRDC. **www.nrdc.org.uk/publications_details.asp?ID=175#**

Crystal, D. (2001) *Language and the Internet.* Cambridge: Cambridge University Press.

Crystal, D. (2005) *How Language Works.* London: Penguin.

Cruttenden, A. (2001) *Gimson's Pronunciation of English, 6th Edition.* London: Arnold.

Ehri, L. C., Nunes, S. R., Stahl, S. A. and Willows, D. M. (2001) 'Systematic phonics instruction helps students learn to read: Evidence from the National Reading Panel's meta-analysis.' *Review of Educational Research*, Vol. 71, No. 3, pp.393–447.

Howard, U. and Kings, P. (eds) (2010) *Why Leadership Matters. Putting basic skills at the heart of adult learning.* London: NRDC.

Hughes, N. and Schwab, I. (2010) *Teaching Adult Literacy. Principles and practice.* London: NRDC.

Mountford, J. (1998) *An insight into English spelling.* London: Hodder & Stoughton.

Roach, P. (2000) *English Phonetics and Phonology: A practical course. 3rd edition.* Cambridge: Cambridge University Press.

Rose, J. (2006) *Independent Review of the Teaching Of Early Reading. Final report.* London: Department for Education and Skills.

Torgerson, C. J., Brooks, G. and Hall, J. (2006) *A Systematic Review of the Research Literature on the Use Of Phonics in the Teaching of Reading and Spelling. DfES research report 711.* London: Department for Education and Skills.
Downloadable from: **http://education.gov.uk/publications/standard/publicationDetail/Page1/RR711**

Glossary

Many of these definitions are based on those in the glossaries in the two Crystal encyclopaedias (1995, 2001). I also refer to other publications, including Roach (2000) and the teachers' notes to *Letters and Sounds*. Some of the terms here can have wider linguistic applications, but I have tried to explain them all in terms of English phonetics and phonics. Where there is another term in bold within a definition it can be found elsewhere within this glossary.

accent Features of pronunciation that signal regional or social identity (cf. **dialect**). Also, emphasis or **stress** given to a spoken word or syllable (but this usage can be confusing and is better avoided).

allophone A variant of a **phoneme**, e.g. 'dark' l at the end of a word or **aspirated** /p/ at the start of a syllable; does not alter the meaning.

alphabetic language A language with a writing system in which a set of symbols (letters, **graphemes**) represents the **phonemes** of the language.

analytic phonics See entry for **phonics**.

articulation The physiological movements involved in modifying a flow of air to produce speech sounds. 'Manner' of articulation is the way in which the flow is modified by degree of closure, to produce, e.g. a **plosive** or **fricative** sound. 'Place' of articulation is where in the vocal tract a speech sound is produced, e.g. **alveolar**, **bilabial**, etc.

aspiration Audible breath or puff of air that may accompany a sound, e.g. /p/ at the start of a syllable ([p^h] in IPA).

alveolar A consonant in which the tongue makes contact with the alveolar ridge (the bony prominence behind the upper teeth), e.g. /t, d, n/.

bilabial A consonant made with both lips together, e.g. /p, b, m/.

blend (in phonics) To build words from their constituent phonemes to read. (Sometimes the word 'blend' is used in the sense of a consonant **cluster**, but this is a use best avoided.)

brackets Conventions used to signal the linguistic status of elements, namely pointed brackets - <pat> - for graphemes and written words, slanted brackets - /pæt/- for phonemes and transcriptions (and for even more detailed phonetic transcriptions, square brackets, e.g. [**p**^{h}æt]).

citation form The form of a linguistic unit when produced in isolation, e.g. a word pronounced carefully on its own, a 'strong' form; cf. **weak form.**

cluster (consonant) A series of adjacent consonants, e.g. /**streŋkθ/** <strength> (which has a three-consonant cluster initially and a three-consonant cluster finally). Not to be confused with the term **blend**, which is sometimes used (inaccurately) with this meaning.

complementary distribution Applies to sounds which have different realisations (forms) depending on where in a word they appear, e.g. in <pip> the initial /p/ is aspirated but final /p/ is not.

correspondence Applies to the relationship that holds between a sound and its written representation (phoneme-grapheme correspondence) or between a grapheme and the sound it represents (grapheme-phoneme correspondence).

decode To decipher and interpret written symbols (graphemes and words) in order to obtain meaning; this can refer more specifically to vocalising words (reading them aloud) or to using phonics to read unknown words.

dental A consonant made by the tongue against the upper teeth. In English, the dental consonants are /θ, ð/.

dialect A language variety in which use of grammar and vocabulary identifies the regional or social background of the user; cf. **accent.**

dialectology The study of regional **dialects**, which can involve the drawing of **isoglosses.**

digraph A two-letter **grapheme** where two letters represent one sound, e.g. digraph <sh> corresponds to /ʃ/.

diphthong A vowel sound in which there is a change of quality – a movement from one vowel to another – during a **syllable**, e.g. <time> /taɪm/**.**

Estuary English An accent of English, with features of London speech, that has spread beyond the Thames Estuary to much of the South-East of England and continues to spread.

fricative A consonant made when two vocal organs come so close together that the air moving between them produces audible friction (hissing noise). In English the fricatives are **/s, z,** ʃ, ʒ, h**/.**

glottal stop See **stop**

grapheme The smallest contrastive unit in the writing system (by analogy with **phoneme**). In literacy terms, the letter or sequence of letters that represents each individual phoneme. See also **digraph** and **trigraph**.

initial Describes the first sound(s) in a word, e.g. in /streŋkθ/ the initial cluster is /str/, and the initial phoneme is /s/.

isogloss A line on a map showing the boundary of an area in which a linguistic feature (of **accent** or **dialect**) is used.

labio-dental A consonant made by contact between the upper teeth and lower lip. The English labio-dental consonants are /f, v/.

larynx Felt or seen as the 'Adam's apple' – the part of the windpipe which contains the **vocal cords**.

'Laura Norder' Famous example of intrusive 'r' – where an /r/ is inserted between vowels. This is how the phrase, 'law and order', sounds with an intrusive 'r' between 'law' and 'and'. (An alternative pronunciation would be to mark the word boundaries with a glottal stop, see **stop**.)

manner of articulation See **articulation.**

medial Describes the sound(s) in the middle of a word; cf. **initial** and **final.**

metalinguistic Describes terminology that is used for talking about language.

minimal pair Words that differ in meaning when only one sound is changed, e.g. /bet/ and /bed/; way of identifying the **phonemes** of a language.

nasal A sound made with the soft palate lowered, thus allowing the air to resonate in the nose; in English the nasal consonants are /m, n, ŋ/.

non-rhotic The opposite of **rhotic.**

phoneme The smallest contrastive unit in the sound system of a language, i.e. the smallest sound that makes a difference of meaning.

phonemic awareness Ability to hear and identify phonemes (a subset of **phonological awareness**).

phonetics The science of speech sounds; articulatory phonetics studies the way speech sounds are produced by the **vocal organs.**

phonics An approach to the teaching of reading and spelling which focuses on the association of phonemes with particular graphemes; **synthetic phonics**, the more frequently used version, involves **sounding out** graphemes and **blending** (synthesising) them for reading, or **segmenting** them for spelling; **analytic phonics** involves no sounding out, but instead word families are studied to work out the patterns.

phonological awareness Awareness of the sound structure of a language.

phonology The study of the sound system, i.e. the way the sounds are organised in a language.

phonotactics The particular sequences of sounds that occur in a language, e.g. in English /spr/ (word-initially) is permitted but /*psr/ is not.

place of articulation See **articulation.**

plosive A consonant made with a complete closure in the **vocal tract**, followed by a sudden release of air ('plosion'). Sometimes known as a **stop** (a term which emphasises the closure).

rhotic accent A variety of accent that pronounces /r/ (where <r> in spelling) after vowels, e.g. <car> /kɑːr/; cf. **non-rhotic** /kɑː/.

received pronunciation (RP) Regionally neutral prestige **accent** of British English, sometimes known as 'BBC English'.

schwa Unstressed vowel transcribed as /ə/. The word is of Hebrew origin, denoting a type of vowel.

segment Break words down into their constituent phonemes to spell.

sound out Say aloud the sound values associated with particular graphemes to help decode words for reading (the preparatory stage to **blending**).

Standard English The 'educated' **dialect** of British English, geographically neutral, used in formal writing.

stop Another word for a **plosive**. Most familiar use is in the expression 'glottal stop', to describe the consonant produced often as a substitute for /t/.

stress The degree of force with which a syllable is uttered. Sometimes known as **accent** (but this confusing usage is to be avoided). A one-beat unit of rhythm, with a vowel (V) as the minimum requirement, with optional consonants (C) before or after, and often different boundary possibilities, e.g. the word <standing> has two syllables, structured either CCVCC + VC or CCVC + CVC. Account is taken of **phonotactics** to help determine boundaries.

synthetic phonics See **phonics.**

trigraph A three-letter grapheme where three letters represent one sound, e.g. trigraph <igh> corresponds to **diphthong** /aɪ/ (as in <light>).

velar A consonant made by the back of the tongue against the soft palate (velum). In English the velar consonants are /g, k, ŋ/.

vocal cords Two muscular folds in the larynx that vibrate as a source of sound, and, in particular, of voicing; sometimes known as vocal folds.

vocal organs The parts of the body involved in the production of speech sounds, e.g. tongue, lips, teeth, soft palate, etc.

vocal tract The whole of the air passage above the **larynx.**

voice, **voicing** The auditory result of vocal cord vibration, producing voiced sounds, e.g. /b, d, g, ʒ, ð/.

weak form The unstressed form of a word in connected speech, e.g. <can> pronounced /kən/ rather than its **citation form** /kæn/.

Appendices

Appendix 1

Table 1: The International Phonetic Alphabet (IPA) symbols for the 24 consonant phonemes of the Received Pronunciation accent of English, with symbols used in *Letters and Sounds* (L&S) where these differ

L&S	IPA		Sample word	IPA transcription
	/b/	as in the first sound of	*buy*	/baɪ/
	/d/	as in the first sound of	*dye*	/daɪ/
	/g/	as in the first sound of	*guy*	/gaɪ/
	/m/	as in the first sound of	*my*	/maɪ/
	/n/	as in the first sound of	*nigh*	/naɪ/
	/p/	as in the first sound of	*pie*	/paɪ/
	/r/	as in the first sound of	*rye*	/raɪ/
	/t/	as in the first sound of	*tie*	/taɪ/
	/k/	as in the first sound of	*coo*	/kuː/
/ch/	/tʃ/	as in the first sound of	*chew*	/tʃuː/
	/f/	as in the first sound of	*few*	/fjuː/
/j/	/dʒ/	as in the first sound of	*jaw*	/dʒɔː/
	/l/	as in the first sound of	*loo*	/luː/
	/s/	as in the first sound of	*sue*	/suː/
	/z/	as in the first sound of	*zoo*	/zuː/
	/v/	as in the first sound of	*view*	/vjuː/
	/h/	as in the first sound of	*who*	/huː/
/ng/	/ŋ/	as in the **last** sound of	*ring*	/rɪŋ/
/sh/	/ʃ/	as in the **third** sound of	*fission*	/'fɪʃən/
/zh/	/ʒ/	as in the **third** sound of	*vision*	/'vɪʒən/
/th/	/θ/	as in the first sound of	*thigh*	/θaɪ/
/**th**/	/ð/	as in the first sound of	*thy*	/ðaɪ/
	/w/	as in the first sound of	*well*	/wel/
/y/	/j/	as in the first sound of	*yell, union*	/jel, 'juːnjən/

Table 2: The International Phonetic Alphabet (IPA) symbols for the 20 vowel phonemes of the Received Pronunciation accent of English, with symbols used in *Letters and Sounds* (L&S) where these differ

L&S	IPA		Sample word	IPA Transcription
/a/	/æ/	as in the first sound of	*ant*	/ænt/
	/e/	as in the first sound of	*end*	/end/
/i/	/ɪ/	as in the first sound of	*ink*	/ɪŋk/
/o/	/ɒ/	as in the first sound of	*ox*	/ɒks/
/u/	/ʌ/	as in the first sound of	*up*	/ʌp/
/oo/	/ʊ/	as in the **second** sound of	*pull*	/pʊl/
	/ə/	('schwa') as in the first sound of	*about*	/ə'baʊt/
/ar/	/ɑː/	as in the first sound of	*aardvark*	/'ɑːdvaːk/
/ur/	/ɜː/	as in the first sound of	*earl*	/ɜːl/
/or/	/ɔː/	as in the **whole** sound of	*awe*	/ɔː/
/ee/	/iː/	as in the first sound of	*eel*	/iːl/
/**oo**/	/uː/	as in the sound of	*ooze*	/uːz/
/ai/	/eɪ/	as in the first sound of	*aim*	/eɪm/
/igh/	/aɪ/	as in the first sound of	*ice*	/aɪs/
/oa/	/əʊ/	as in the first sound of	*oath*	/əʊθ/
/ow/	/aʊ/	as in the first sound of	*ouch*	/aʊtʃ/
/oi/	/ɔɪ/	as in the first sound of	*oyster*	/'ɔɪstə/
/ai/	/eə/	as in the **whole** sound of	*air*	/eə/
/ear/	/ɪə/	as in the **whole** sound of	*ear*	/ɪə/
/ure/	/ʊə/	as in the **second** sound of	*juror*	/'dʒʊərə/

Appendix 2

The 'English phonemic alphabet' from the Glossary to the Core Curriculum: **www.excellencegateway.org.uk/sflcurriculum**

Phonemic alphabet

The English phonemic alphabet includes the 46 distinctive sounds (phonemes) of the English language.

Consonants

p	pen	/pen/	s	see	/siː/
b	bad	/bæd/	z	zoo	/zuː/
t	tea	/tiː/	ʃ	shoe	/ʃuː/
d	did	/dɪd/	ʒ	vision	/'vɪʒn/*
k	cat	/kæt/	h	hat	/hæt/
g	get	/get/	m	man	/mæn/
ʧ	chain	/ʧeɪn/	n	now	/naʊ/
ʤ	jam	/ʤæm/	ŋ	sing	/sɪŋ/
f	fall	/fɔːl/	l	leg	/leg/
v	van	/væn/	r	red	/red/
θ	thin	/θɪn/	j	yes	/jes/
ð	this	/ðɪs/	w	wet	/wet/

Vowels and diphthongs

iː	see	/siː/	ʌ	cup	/kʌp/
i	happy	/'hæpi/**	ɜː	fur	/fɜː(r)/
ɪ	sit	/sɪt/	ə	about	/ə'baʊt/
e	ten	/ten/	eɪ	say	/seɪ/
æ	cat	/kæt/	əʊ	go	/gəʊ/
ɑː	father	/'fɑːðə(r)/	aɪ	my	/maɪ/
ɒ	got	/gɒt/	ɔɪ	boy	/bɔɪ/
ɔː	saw	/sɔː/	aʊ	now	/naʊ/
ʊ	put	/pʊt/	ɪə	near	/nɪə(r)/
u	actual	/'æktʃuəl/**	eə	hair	/heə(r)/
uː	too	/tuː/	ʊə	pure	/pjʊə(r)/

Additional notes on the 'Phonemic alphabet' from *Excellence Gateway*:

* /n/ in /'vɪʒn/ should be marked as syllabic – /ˌ/ – otherwise this word would more accurately be transcribed as /'vɪʒən/ since it does not consist of a single syllable.

** It is unusual to list short /i u/ as phonemes of English in addition to /iː uː/. It would be difficult to find contexts in which they are actually contrastive (the definition of phoneme). Note also that the final sound of <happy> is pronounced /ɪ/ in some accents of English. <Actual> may not be the best illustration of /u/ as there could be confusion with /ʊə/, or there may be no /u/ as the word can also be pronounced /'æktʃəl/.

Appendix 3

Lists of phoneme–grapheme and grapheme-phoneme correspondences

Table 1: The phoneme–grapheme correspondences of British English spelling, by RP phoneme: Consonants

Phoneme	Grapheme(s)		As in ...	Common words with rare graphemes for the phoneme
	Basic	Other		
/b/	b	bb	bed rabbit	<bu> buy
/k/	c	ck k q ch	come back look queen Christmas	<cu> biscuit
/tʃ/	ch	tch	children match	<t> picture
/d/	d	dd ed	dad teddy called	
/f/	f	ff ph	from off elephant	<gh> cough enough laugh rough tough
/g/	g	gg	get jogging	<gh> ghost <gu> guy
/h/	h		horse	<wh> who whole
/dʒ/	j	dg dge g ge	just budgie bridge giant orange	

/l/	l	ll	leg ball	
/m/	m	mm	my mummy	<mb> climb lamb thumb <me> come some <mn> autumn
/n/	n	nn	now dinner	<ne> done engine none <kn> knife knot know
/ŋ/	ng	n	sing sink	
/p/	p	pp	pen apple	<ph> shepherd
/r/	r	rr	red berry	<wr> write
/s/	s	c ce se ss	sit city once horse grass	<st> castle Christmas listen
/ʃ/	sh	ti	ship station	<ch> machine <ci> special <s> sugar sure <ssi> permission
/ʒ/	si		vision	<s> treasure usual
/t/	t	tt ed	but little looked	<th> Thomas <tw> two
/θ/	th		thing	
/ð/	th		that	<the> breathe
/v/	v	ve	very have	<f> of
/w/	w	u	went queen	<wh> what when (etc.) /wʌ/ spelt <o> once one
/j/	y		yellow	<i> onion
/z/	z	s se ze zz	zoo is please sneeze puzzle	<ss> scissors

Table 2: The phoneme–grapheme correspondences of British English spelling, by RP phoneme: Vowels

Phoneme	Grapheme(s)		As in …	Common words with rare graphemes for the phoneme
	Basic	Other		
/æ/	a		and	
/ə/	a	e er o	about the butter button	<ar> sugar <i> possible <our> colour <re> centre <ure> picture
/eɪ/	a.e	a ai ay	came bacon paint day	<aigh> straight <ea> break great <eigh> eight <ey> they
/eə/	air	are ar	fair fare parent	<ear> bear pear tear wear <ere> there where <eir> their
/ɑː/	ar	a	far ask	<al> half <are> are <au> aunt laugh <ear> heart
/e/	e	ea	went bread	<a> any many <ai> said <ay> says <ie> friend
/iː/	ee	e ea ey ie y	see he beach key field city	<e.e> these <eo> people
/ɪə/	eer	ear er ere	cheer hear hero here	<ier> fierce
/ɜː/	er	ir or ur	her girl worm fur	<ear> early earth heard learn <ere> were <our> journey
/ɪ/	i	e y	is England gym	<a> sausage
/aɪ/	i.e	i igh y	like I night my	<eigh> height <eye> eye /aɪe/ spelt <ir, ire, yre> biro fire tyre

/ɒ/	o	a	not was	<au> because sausage <ou> cough
/əʊ/	o	o.e ow	so bone blow	<oa> boat <oh> oh
/ɔɪ/	oi	oy	boil boy	
/ʊ/	oo	u	book put	<oul> could should would
/uː/	oo	ew u u.e	too blew super rule	<oe> shoe <o> do to two who <ou> you <ough> through <ue> blue <ui> fruit
/ʊə/	oor	ure	poor sure	<our> tour
/ɔː/	or	a ar au aw ore	for all warn sauce saw before	<augh> caught naughty <oor> door floor <ough> bought <our> four your
/aʊ/	ou	ow	out down	/aʊə/ spelt <our, ower> flour flower
/ʌ/	u	o	but some	<ou> country young /wʌ/ spelt <o> once one

Table 3: The phoneme-grapheme correspondences of British English spelling: Two-phoneme sequences frequently spelt with single graphemes

Two-phoneme sequence	Grapheme(s)		As in …	Two-grapheme spellings for same sequence
	Basic	Other		
/əl/ (only word-final)	le		little	anim**al** lab**el** penc**il** car**ol** beautif**ul**
/juː/	u	ew ue u.e	union few argue cute	v**iew** **you**
/ks/	x		box	ban**ks** tri**cks** politi**cs**

Note: The two-phoneme sequence /kw/ is almost always spelt <qu> and should also be taught as a unit.

Table 4: The grapheme-phoneme correspondences of British English spelling: Single graphemes frequently pronounced as two-phoneme sequences

Grapheme(s)	Two-phoneme sequence	Other phonemes	As in …
ew u ue u.e	/juː/	(too many to list)	few union argue cute
le (only word-final)	/əl/		little
x	/ks/		box

Note: The two-grapheme sequence <qu> is almost always pronounced/ kw/ and should be taught as a unit.

Table 5: The grapheme–phoneme correspondences of British English spelling: Major correspondences for consonants

Grapheme(s)	Phoneme(s)		As in ...
	Basic	Other	
b bb	/b/		bed rabbit
c	/k/	/s/	come city
ce	/s/		once
ch	/tʃ/	/k/	children Christmas
ck	/k/		back
d dd	/d/		dad teddy
dg(e)	/dʒ/		budgie bridge
ed	/d/	/t/	called looked
f ff	/f/		from off
g	/g/	/dʒ/	get giant
ge	/dʒ/		orange
gg	/g/		jogging
h	/h/		horse
j	/dʒ/		just
k	/k/		look
l ll	/l/		leg ball
m mm	/m/		my mummy
n	/n/	/ŋ/	now sink
ng	/ŋ/		sing
nn	/n/		dinner
p pp	/p/		pen apple
ph	/f/		elephant
q	/k/		queen
r rr	/r/		red berry
s se	/s/	/z/	sit is horse please
sh	/ʃ/		ship
si	/ʒ/		vision
ss	/s/		grass
t tt	/t/		but little
tch	/tʃ/		match
th	/θ/	/ð/	thing that
ti	/ʃ/		station

u	/w/		queen
v ve	/v/		very have
w	/w/		went
y	/j/		yellow
z ze zz	/z/		zoo sneeze puzzle

Table 6: The grapheme-phoneme correspondences of British English spelling: Minor correspondences for consonants

Grapheme(s)	Phoneme(s)	As in ...
bu	/b/	buy
ch ci	/ʃ/	machine special
cu	/k/	biscuit
f	/v/	of
gh	/f g/	cough enough laugh rough tough; ghost
gu	/g/	guy
i	/j/	onion
kn	/n/	knife knot know
mb me mn	/m/	climb lamb thumb; come some; autumn
ne	/n/	done engine none
o	/wʌ/	once one
ph	/p/	shepherd
s ssi	/ʃ/	sugar sure; permission
s	/ʒ/	treasure usual
ss	/z/	scissors
st	/s/	castle Christmas listen
t	/tʃ/	picture
th tw	/t/	Thomas two
the	/ð/	breathe
wh	/h w/	who whole; what when (etc.)
wr	/r/	write

Table 7: The grapheme–phoneme correspondences of British English spelling: Major correspondences for vowels

Grapheme(s)	Phoneme(s)		As in …
	Basic	Other	
a	/æ/	/eɪ ɑː ɒ ɔː ə/	and bacon ask was all about
a.e ai ay	/eɪ/		came paint day
air are	/eə/		fair fare
ar	/ɑː/	/eə ɔː/	far parent warn
au aw	/ɔː/		sauce saw
e	/e/	/iː ɪ ə/	went he England the
ea	/iː/	/e/	beach bread
ear eer ere	/ɪə/		hear cheer here
ee ey	/iː/		see key
er	/ɜː/	/ɪə ə/	her hero butter
ew	/uː/		blew
i	/ɪ/	/aɪ/	is I
ie	/iː/		field
i.e igh	/aɪ/		like night
ir	/ɜː/		girl
o	/ɒ/	/ʌ əʊ ə/	not some so button
o.e	/əʊ/		bone
oi oy	/ɔɪ/		boil boy
oo	/uː/	/ʊ/	too book
oor	/ɔː/	/ʊə/	door poor
or	/ɔː/	/ɜː/	for worm
ore	/ɔː/		before
ou	/aʊ/		out
ow	/aʊ/	/əʊ/	down blow
u	/ʌ/	/ʊ uː/	but put super
u.e	/uː/		rule
ur	/ɜː/		fur
y	/aɪ/	/ɪ iː/	my gym city

Table 8: The grapheme–phoneme correspondences of British English spelling: Minor correspondences for vowels

Grapheme(s)	Phoneme(s)	As in …
a	/e ɪ/	any many; sausage
ai ay	/e/	said; says
aigh	/eɪ/	straight
al are	/ɑː/	half; are
ar	/ə/	sugar
au	/ɑː ɒ/	aunt laugh; because sausage
augh	/ɔː/	caught naughty
ea ey	/eɪ/	break great; they
ear	/eə ɑː ɜː/	bear pear tear wear; heart; early earth heard learn
e.e eo	/iː/	these; people
eigh	/eɪ aɪ/	eight; height
eir	/eə/	their
ere	/eə ɜː/	there where; were
eye	/aɪ/	eye
i	/ə/	possible
ie	/e/	friend
ier	/ɪə/	fierce
ir ire	/aɪə/	biro fire
o	/wʌ/	once one
o oe	/uː/	do to two who; shoe
oa oh	/əʊ/	boat oh
oor	/ɔː/	door floor
ou	/ɒ uː ʌ/	cough; you; country young
ough	/uː ɔː/	through; bought
oul	/ʊ/	could should would
our	/ə ɜː ʊə ɔː aʊə/	colour; journey; tour; four your; flour
ower	/aʊə/	flower
re	/ə/	centre
ue ui	/uː/	blue fruit
ure	/ə/	picture
yre	/aɪə/	tyre